Proverbs

15 Key Verses for children
from the book of Proverbs

**BIBLE CHAPTERS
FOR KIDS**

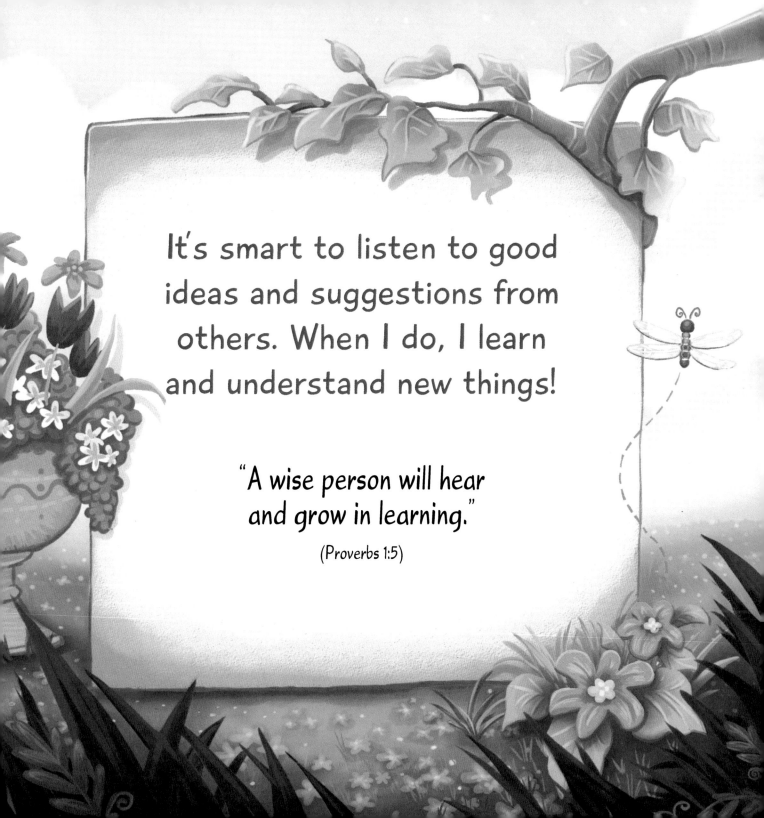

It's smart to listen to good ideas and suggestions from others. When I do, I learn and understand new things!

"A wise person will hear and grow in learning."

(Proverbs 1:5)

Respecting God and His Word is the first step in growing up to be wise.

"The fear of the Lord is the beginning of wisdom. but foolish people turn away from it."

(Proverbs 1:7)

God's Word teaches me about doing the right things. I want to do what it tells me, with my whole heart.

"Do not forget my law; let your heart keep my commandments."

(Proverbs 3:1)

I trust in God with my whole heart. I don't have to figure everything out on my own, because He knows what's best for me. I pray that He will help me to make good choices.

"Trust in the Lord with all your heart and He will guide you in His ways."

(Proverbs 3:5,6)

When my mind thinks about good things, I am happy and kind.

"Keep your heart clean."

(Proverbs 4:23a)

I can choose to do good or bad. It pleases God and others when I stay away from doing bad things.

"Keep away from evil."

(Proverbs 4:27)

God blesses me when I
share and give to others.
I feel good when I think
about others and it makes
them happy too.

"A sharing person
will be blessed."

(Proverbs 11:25)

I need to work hard and faithfully every day. It's not always easy, but I am proud when I see a job well done, and I feel God's blessing.

"In all work there is a reward."

(Proverbs 14:23)

Because I want to be a real friend, I should be loving all the time, and not only when I want something in return.

"A friend shows love at all times."

(Proverbs 17:17)

0.80 $

Ice Cream

Ice Cream

When I answer others with a gentle voice, it helps take angry feelings away. But if I answer in a mean way, it makes the angry feelings grow.

"A kind word turns away anger."

(Proverbs 15:1a)

When I talk to others in a kind way, they will want to be sweet and nice in return.

"Kind words are sweet, like honey."

(Proverbs 16:24)

It's best to be honest, because God knows everything. He sees when I do the right thing, and He also sees when I do wrong.

"The eyes of the Lord are everywhere."

(Proverbs 15:3)

When I pray and ask for God's help in what I'm doing, things go much better for me.

"Give your plans to the Lord and you will do well."

(Proverbs 16:3)

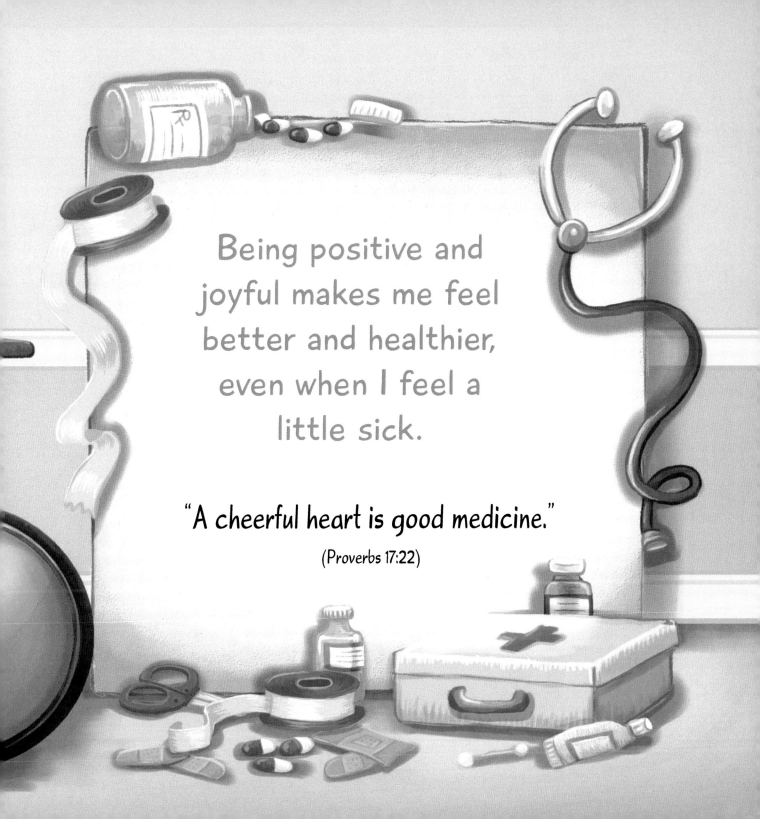

Being positive and joyful makes me feel better and healthier, even when I feel a little sick.

"A cheerful heart is good medicine."

(Proverbs 17:22)

I want to learn as much as I can now, so that when I am old, I can be smart and wise.

"Get all the advice and instruction you can, so you will be wise in your old age."

(Proverbs 19:20)

More books in the series:

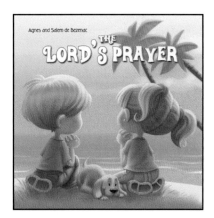
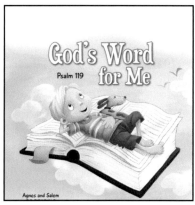

iCHARACTER

Published by iCharacter Ltd. (Ireland)
www.iCharacter.org
By Agnes and Salem de Bezenac
Illustrated by Agnes de Bezenac
Colored by Noviyanti W.
Copyright. All rights reserved.
All Bible verses adapted from the KJV.

Made in the USA
Middletown, DE
06 January 2022